_sandpaperkisses

Letters Lamenting A Living Lilith

Kenny| Kenzo| DeMarlo

This is a work of fiction. Names, characters, places, and incidents either are the product of the author's imagination or are used fictitiously. Any resemblance to actual persons, living or dead, events, or locales is entirely coincidental.

Copyright © 2020 by Kenneth D. R. Coleman

All rights reserved. No part of this book may be reproduced or used in any manner without written permission of the copyright owner except for the use of quotations in a book review. For more information, address: kennethsunyacoleman@gmail.com.

First paperback edition November 2020

Book design by Kenneth D. R. Coleman

ISBN 978-0-578-72193-4

for C'Èra— Lilith, my Goddess. the woman who is muse for this magnum opus. let these unanswered prayers become sacrificial lamb for my selfish healing; pimping out my trauma— you are the sun: reflecting your light— i shine now.

i love you.

PLAYLIST

DEMARLO'S ARC: DEVIL'S DESCENT

Track 0: Preface or lack there of?
Track 1: Petals
Track 2: Dreams
Track 3: Trapped is My Nest
Track 4: Casí777
Track 5: Leviathan
Track 6: star-crossed scars
Track 7: Apocrypha: This Must Be The Wrong Timeline— Take Me To A Different Isekai
Track 8: Chembur 'li Phroust
Track 9: Face
Track 10: Bottomless
Track 11: Loneliness
Track 12: Damn, She Smells Good AF!
Track 13: Stxxl
Track 14: Ghost Town. Heart. Miscommunication
Track 15: Rage In a Vacuum
Track 16: Possession
Shinigami Interlude (pt. 1)
Track 17: She said, "I have no idea what you're doing out all day when you're coming home this late"
Track 18: Black Boy with the Greenest Eyes
Track 19: Prosperity
Track 20: I know I piss a lot of people off but that's y'all problem, not mine lol
Track 21: Black Boy Power Ranger
Track 22: Crystal Healing

KENNY'S ARC: SERAPHIM SPARRING

Track 23: And Depression Comes Marching In
Track 24: "you know what? I'm dope as fuck"
Track 25: Black Boy in Patchwork
Shinigami Interlude (pt. 2)
Track 26: Gessy 'mae
Track 27: yeah, umm no
Track 28: The 10 Commandments of Respecting Kenny
Track 29: Downfall
Track 30: Hoarder
Track 31: My Soul is a Shipwreck
1st Requiem: Eternal
Track 32: Frozen
Track 33: Hoarse
Track 34: How To Mold A Muse
Track 35: Water Bending
Track 36: black boy plucks petals in the rain
Track 37: psycho-self-mutilation
Track 38: The Theatre of Sorrowful Sloth
Track 39: Melding, I'm Melting
Track 40: Fate Plotted My Torment
Track 41: Morning Dew
Track 42: To:
Track 43: Mourning Melodies
Track 44: Elevate
Track 45: Lover's Block

Kenzo's Arc: Amaranthine Amalgam

Shinigami Interlude (pt. 3)
Track 46: if you ever wonder why I'm silent.
Track 47: DeMarlo's Lullaby
Track 48: Phantom (Kenzo)
Track 49: Bonds & Severing
Track 50: she asked to be my reason for writing but that's impossible. the spot is already taken.
Track 51: Cinders
Track 52: WindScar|Hearts
Track 53: Smōak
Track 54: Chrysalis
Track 55: C r o w d   C o n t r o l l
Track 56: Forethought
Track 57: Leap, nigga!
Track 58: mis. understood
Track 59: DeMarlo?
Track 60: Lilacs for Lilith
Track 61: I loved you first, *sticks tongue out

Final Requiem: _sandpaperkisses
Bonus Track 1: you're so damn stoic, it makes me sick
Bonus Track 2: flooded her Pearly Gates—now you babble in ruins like a Tower of Babel
Bonus Track 3: incomplete
Bonus Track 4: Letting Silence Bleed Onto Others

Preface or lack there of?

poetry for me is usually protest. storytelling that carries a message to ignite change. a voice for the voiceless. a craft with the power to teach. but this isn't that. this is something personal. out of my comfort zone. without form or structure. a loss of ethics. my voice.

there's no big philosophical realization or direction in sight. I'm just trying to convey how aimless. uncertain. endless. and how repetitive life can be. I'm hurt. can't let go. bitter. depressed. full of angst and anxiety. feeling like I'm not good enough while dealing with a new person every now and then. I'm not seeking pity. I willingly am this broken record. I have glimpses of changing this desolate reality for myself but that's something that seemingly always slips my grasp.

DeMarlo's Arc: Devil's Descent

Petals

subtracting possibilities

by thousands like counting
paper cranes

tying the
knot?

she loves me.

not.

Dreams

my dreams are bittersweet

temporary. highs of happiness.
memories.lingering.aromas
of brown sugar and cinnamon. held
within her arms, sinking in
a place where my rage is calmed

for a moment
it feels so real   then
        surreal

      like making a deal with a devil
         my   demons
         conjure up this lie
         a sweet matrix to indulge in
         her fingers dig into my ribs

            "don't let go"
            "don't let go"
            "don't.

              go!"

Trapped Is My Nest

it's hard not to feel trapped when the
world thinks you made it out

but you just regular
you copped that
piece of paper

and you still nigga

they called you the miracle,
the golden child
but in the mirror
all you see is pyrite

brittle and bitter
with your broken heart
worn on a torn sleeve

that drips a *Sanguine
Paradise*. melancholy
is your street style of self
inflicted wounds

you're such a stagnant
stallion. so sheltered,
wet behind the ears
should've snipped
the excess away years ago

maybe your skin would be thicker
maybe your star wouldn't dim

and flicker
a broken constellation
befallen as you wither

forgotten.

Casí777

dead rose emoji— black heart aesthetic:

she's a stallion
rocking faux locs
down to her hips
like Medusa

Comme des Garçons
tatted on her face
with the heartbreak
she likes 808s
Cudi, Trippie and Kanye

She be Murakami with the
paint brush, punk
pop culture yet she's such a loner
everything with her is "almost"
a holy grail half-full
yet at any time
she's liable to go ghost

what can Kenny say— emotionally unavailable
is my type of woman

Levitation

we sailed through desert sea
through heaven and hell
until she ghosted her shell
and shipwrecked mine

I watched a Siren shed her
skin, evolve
into a Leviathan
with such grace
yet malice
uses silence
as her weapon
her Gjallarhorn
to sound off
deep within my psyche
where Ragnarok became
Rapture. the killing of a god
from a goddess: my ego
caught in her waves
as she waves goodbye

it hurts to lose an anchor

star-crossed scars

lonely and upset
the pot calls the kettle
black
hole
glutton
starved yet
filled to the brim
with regrets

color pallet be nighted
an armor where every star
forms a constellation of scars
on melanated body

Apocrypha: This Must Be The Wrong Timeline— Take Me To A Different Isekai

every time I stare at a blank page
I'm reminded of the emptiness I feel

as thoughts begin to form
tears as warm as her touch
begin to boil at the surface
of my eyelids
metaphors become poisons
and tragedies for a drunken hero
drifting off
my hubris

dammit
I'm falling
into writing
about the same shit
again
I hate it

how the hell
am I supposed to heal
when I find foam-like
comfort in this pain
attached to every memory
like they be my ligaments
I hoard them like Fafnir

treasure them within
a cloud on my
Apple cellular

I feel a wave of shame
every time I take a bite
of megabytes; my eyes open up
to every megapixel
where her smile
comes to life

melts my heart
still gives me butterflies
that I want to hate
so much
but I guess this be the
butterfly effect
chaos theory
because my life is post
apocalyptic

black boy collected
the chaos emeralds
and fucked up the timeline

Chembur 'li Phroust

falling in love
feels a lot like
falling in ruin

like Lucy falling
right into
my arms

I cannot tell
if her smile
is wicked

or if she is
genuinely into me
why would an angel

dig someone as
unholy as me
if she was not

sent to leave
me six feet
under

Face

you handle yourself
without care

obsessed with how
unfair loss is

you become lifeless
shades of grey

and not the thrilling
shades of ambiguity

but a rain cloud reigning
his own terror

an addict for agony
you are witness

to your anagnorisis.
how will you reset

and re-reverse this
without looking back?

you willfully become a pillar
of salt everyday

it is insanity
that you expect

change. you are a one
note climate. a caterpillar

stuck in the storm afraid
of his own cocoon

afraid of the goo
you would become

you put on a face
crack your warmest

smile. ashamed to show
your only weakness

you don't want anyone to worry

so you carry all
the weight

by yourself hidden
behind the face yearning

to move forward
to move past Fear

Bottomless

depression is
an ocean
with no end

we drink to it
until bottled-up
emotions come
spewing out

you'd think we'd
drown by now within
the currents. stuck in the
past, we've adapted

this is evolution
as we breathe
inhale the toxins
this is addiction

to the anguish because
tears are routine now.
like clockwork
on a broken clock

we know it's wrong
at least we can be right
twice a day

Loneliness

have you ever rode the train
with tears across your face
with one snotty nostril
that you've tasted at least
twice but at this point
you couldn't care less

the saltiness is somewhat
sweet. it doesn't disrupt
your immersion of this torment
but at least it's something
that doesn't hurt you

it's warm like the tears you
hold on to. sometimes
they burn but it feels
so good. this is how
we self harm. emotional
scars and wounds we
reopen every time
we revisit memories

Damn, She Smells Good AF!

vanilla sugar
her aura. warm. held tightly
safe within her arms

Stxxl

frost bitten stillness
anxiety steals your time
learn to steel your heart

Ghost Town. Heart. Miscommunication

destiny seems like
desolate Desdemona
my self destruction

Rage In a Vacuum

rage is a
bottled up
vacuum
where flames
disperse
into nothingness

an emptiness
where misery
has no host
to confide in

so it rages
to its heart's content
endless
never satisfied
hopeless

wishing on stars
that never took off
you should've known
star-crossed
meant bad luck

now you're fucked up
that black magic
backfired
left you cursed
deprived of an anchor

that kept you high
you should've known
rose colored lenses
come with thorns
on the frames

you should have
sharpened your fangs
instead you wallow
and weep
in bittersweet
torment

Possession

'never played with a ouija board
but going through a lover's phone and
possessions
are just as   dangerous

insecurities take possession over Kenny
that ain't him no more
that's anxiety
he's Sasuke-salty   after a battle on
                                   the rooftop

he's a cool cat
                         on a hot tin
                         rooftop

he can't weather this change in climate

he's ready to die

                               off
                               like saber tooth

               but insecurities
           possess him
                  like a marionette

           pull his threads
               and he'll

             pick up
                  her phone

Kermit's silhouette

                  on his shoulders
            whispers,   "do it"

            he enters passcode
         to swipe through widow's threads

      "—that lack of trust gone
       leave you widowed, nigga"

Shinigami Interlude (pt. 1)

have you ever had a shinigami
follow you like rain clouds

in the darkest of hours
I make two-hour
commutes by train

it's storming
and I hate the rain
but on days like this
I let it ravage me
drenched in heavenly
piss to hide my tears

as if the fog on
my glasses
wasn't enough

usually I'm prissy
but depression has
me out here careless

muddy in my good shoes
oddly, the city is beautiful
through murky vision
at midnight
how traffic lights
and headlights
blend together

to form cosmic galaxies
on this concrete jungle
it's beautiful

the blur becomes
its own acid trip
through galleries
and I'm searching
and searching
for every meaning
of this abstraction

yet it's empty

She said, *"I have no idea what you're doing out all day when you're coming home this late"*

while you spent days at work
I
ran the city
like I
moved work

all I
got is my voice
and these poems
so I
had to sell myself
with every pitch

every evening I
found a stage to
casket
before clocking
into graveyard
shifts

it really hurt when
you called me, "hot"
for that

I

do admit I
was self absorbed with my
own ambitions,

leaving you in the dark
with every last-second
decision I
made. I

never considered your feelings
on my outings. I

really do wing the fuck out of life
it's an Endless Waltz. I
was living for the moment
trying to live out my dreams—

"one day I'll get paid for this"

make the world my turf
and canvas it

"The Kenny World Tour"

you like Italian? I
would show the real Italy
and you could watch me
soar like shooting star
and rock stages across oceans

Black Boy with the Greenest Eyes

he's become a dormant
Adonis
hiding behind adornments
of a broken heart
he has dreams to rival
the likes of Apollo
to one day swallow
the sun itself
like emerald coated lion
he wants a deconstruction
of every roaming titan
who has an iron grip
on this industry
call it renaissance
Ragnarok for dinosaurs
Neon Guts his ambiance
lately it's been hard for him
to find his glow
what was internal star
seems more like mirror rock
reflecting solar rays in the dark
like replica
he wonders has he missed his mark
as he wanders the midnight
of this underworld with ravens
ribbed to his aura
that remind him of the despair

he carries
swallows his melancholy like candy
because it reminds him of sweeter
days before bitterness
devoured him whole
his heart
empty abyss
a black hole
full of depression
a dense regret
that lingers on his soul
like magnet
he feels stagnant
takes a hiatus
to heal
but it feels
like failure
to watch as his peers
grow without him
so selfish
he doesn't
want them
to outgrow him
he's afraid
they might
abandon
him

too

he cries sea foam
that spawns Aphrodite-demons
they grant him eyes as green
as emeralds
he knows he should sage
but instead he masters
Sage Mode
knows he can't control
his demons
so he guides them
in Reconstruction
making sure it's perfect
so there won't be any New Deal
with a devil

he transmutes jealousy
into passion
his heart into coal
fossil
fuel for his ambitions
awakening of a giant
Adonis with eyes of
moss midnight
he has a goal
to trample upon
the Apollos
with his contemporaries
black boys with
the greenest eyes
becomes the most
ambitious of men

Prosperity

lately, I've been manifesting
hoping these seeds planted
grow into fruition
as I water my words
to form spells
that rival rivers
I'm breaking the levees
of life with these poems
no longer a caged bird
to the depression
that hugs my soul
with a tight grip
I know I walk a tightrope
with my demons
but I let them meet
my angels
we form bonds in balance
seek pleasures and abundance
I commit to my talents
soon, we'll be in business
no longer a mourning
star
I'll rock my halo with the horns happily
call it a thorny crown
as I prosper
the young grasshopper
bound by no gravity
you see it in my roots
how it floats

life for me will be beers and skittles
I prefer cheap wine and pink starburst
but you get the picture
I'm ready to taste the love of my life
let her know that my tongue
is well versed
turn this literature
into gold
just to give back
to the hood
I want these poems
to heal my people too
move them further into
their power
remind them we are beings of light
and love
gloved in melanin
whole
as we vibrate
with the highest frequencies of
the universe

lately, I've been manifesting
hoping these seeds I've planted
grow into fruition

I know I piss a lot of people off but that's y'all problem, not mine lol

Ken— bleached hair like Kaneki
choker chained 'round my neck
with the black denim jacket, yeah
it's cropped
you out the picture now, haha I
move how I
want
straight out of limbo
middle of the night Links
like I
got Synchros, Exceeds— nah,

expectations

I
subvert them. submerged
in uncertainty— I
am such a doll, Ken
when I
finally paint my nails
obsidian to match my heart

I
will be dripped in oil
fossil fuel
ahead of my time

yet I
still feel so much behind...

fuck it. I
do what the fuck I
want because I
am dope as fuck

Black Boy Power Ranger

let this be
coal for your engine
on the railway
so we can morph
into Light Speed

Rescue
our people
like the heroes
we were born to be

we will no longer
live in the limbo
of a Lost Galaxy

through a Time
Force we'll undergo
Primal Reversion

get in tuned
with our Wild Force
like Sage Mode
and soon we'll
whip up a Ninja
Storm

we drum
to the beat of a
Dino Thunder

a black nationalist
Jungle Fury
type beat

we make sure to keep
that Ninja Steel
on our waists
in the form of a
second amendment

just for protection
don't make us shift
into Turbo

we might leave
you in Space

Crystal Healing

when I gave you my first amethyst
I expected you to cherish it
not like an engagement ring
but still
something of utter importance
just another way to share waves
of my energy through
long distances

something for you to hold onto tightly
when you would miss me
the crystal would bleed
shattered fragments of my soul
feeding you samples
of my essence
vampire
succubus
you already had my style
I loved when you wore my clothes
you said my scent made you feel safe
yours made me feel the same
a warm vanilla sugar that cradled
and calmed the storms
of my anxiety

I miss it
you left me nothing of yours
just this clear quartz
you bought me to replace

the amethyst you lost
a year and a half too late

this crystal never carried
pieces of you
it was just a departing gift
wrapped in counterfeit
sentiments

it doesn't carry any traits
of the soul that once
showered me with the most
abundant love
it's just a void
like how you are an avoidant
nonchalant abyss
of a goddess
who never answers
prayers

why is my lament so eternal?
is this what religion feels like?

to put your naked trust into someone
to give them your bare heart
only for them to leave scars upon it
like branding
of course the pain was scorching
for months you heard my screaming
cries and howling
at every full moon

because it pulls me
like Tide when I'm weeping
yet it never cleansed
my dirty laundry

but I guess
you don't owe me a damned thing
and I know
I'm just lonely and upset
using a lost amethyst
to make you subject
to my butt-hurt criticism

it's just that
the other day
I came across a scent
so close to yours
that for a brief moment
my anxiety subsided

and I felt safe.

Kenny's Arc: Seraphim Sparring

And Depression Comes Marching In

when you think you've beaten your depression

here it comes again like Jessie and James
to remind you
that productivity is not a bandaid
that escapism and anime
are not therapy
you cannot Edo Tensei
a dead relationship
Kenny
dead ends only bring you dead ends
that split down the root
and we don't want that

do we?

it's bad for your hair and your health
but we couldn't care less

it's hard to give a fuck about life
when you can't have who you
desire most
when you can longer turn over and hold
her in your arms
she's no longer your steel beams
for support
you out here trying to play Romeo
and drove that dagger

like aircraft
into your chest
nigga, you sabotaged that

I really did

I said she had weapons of
mass destruction in every
poem I've written
titled her, *"terrorist"*
I formed words into propaganda
to paint her villain

but the truth is
I'm just bitter, and salty
like the corner store food
that's slowly killing me
salty as every time
I look back to revisit
memories I wish
I'd let go of
I turn into a skyscraper
of salt

and it's because I know
I lost a rarity
like that five-star jpeg wiafu
on rate up that breaks the game
my Cleo in this Lost Dragalia
I'm Ikki with a lost Regalia

there you go again making object
out of a woman

but how else can I describe
how much this woman
be a treasure

she was always thoughtful
you know it's love
when she put
food on my plate
every time I looked away
into the distance and spaced out
I hated the pain
when she would pop the bumps
on my face
but I was hers
and she made me feel safe
I always say
that her presence
calmed the storms
of my anxiety
she kept me anchored
feeling appreciated
and wanted
she was my biggest fan
the first to all my shows
and the first to see the
darkest roots of my soul
I remember crying in her
solar beaming arms
as I shedded childhood trauma
like snake's skins

exposed my monster within
with the greenest eyes yet,
still she accepted me
for all of my madness
and every time I think
I've gotten over her

my depression comes marching in again
like Jessie and James

to remind me…

"you know what? I'm dope as fuck"

she slid in my inbox
and I was like yooooo
she's dope as fuck—
what the fuck
she sees in me?

I'm just Kenny
still trying to figure out life
because it feels stagnant
like a still image
I thought a degree would make things
picture perfect
but it's all a blur

I'm still grateful though
I'd do it all over again
maybe apply myself more

I just can't help but be a Slifer Slacker
like Jaden
I'm a Misfit
I've always been an outsider
yet I'm the center of the cypher circle

they have their expectations
but my silhouette doesn't fit the
preconceived image

I didn't become the ball player
or the doctor,
the lawyer
or the engineer
I severed STEM
the moment
I decided on performance
and put faith in my pen

sometimes I wonder
if that was the wrong decision

maybe that's just my depression talking
I lost the love of my life
now anxiety haunts my broken heart like a
haunted house
I've been living a play within a play
like The Mouse Trap
—a seemingly blind boy
trapped within inertia
who loves taking cat naps
to escape reality
because living
feels a lot
like agony
when I'm stuck
in the past

lately I've been moving forward
cutting cords, moving towards

my power like I pulled the sword, Excalibur
no longer in a cage
now I practice Sage Mode
to sage ghost

cleansing up my lifestyle
I still keep Angels as ammo
while restoring balance within myself
like Zuko
I'm fire bending, breathing life
dragon dancing, sunny day
like Sozin's Comet
solar beaming, watch me shine
I aged in that cellar with my demons
long enough like wine
petra stella
interstellar
I'll always be a rockstar
so far, I Manifest Destiny
like a conqueror
yet I'm still searching
trying to figure out adulting

she slid in my inbox
and I was like yooooo
she's dope as fuck—
what the fuck
she sees in me?

I'm just Kenny
but I'm pretty dope

Black Boy in Patchwork

you in my corner
was all the affirmation
I needed to know that
I was destined
for greatness

you made me feel strong
no longer alone
on this road where the
irregularity of my
profession composes
a future so uncertain

you were my only certainty
a compass, an anchor, a form
of emotional security
you accepted me
for this beautiful
mess that I am

and I'm not the
type to seek
anyone's
approval. I just know
that I am an acquired
taste

like

how can a nigga so sweet
be cis–gendered
how can a nigga so timid
command such presence
so soft spoken yet
violently thunderous
silences audiences

shit

it still surprises me
that I get people to cry
and witness catharsis

black boy with "Bleach" hair
like Ichigo, Hollow chest
sad boy, triple X,
dressed in emo— grunge
a little androgynous, Flyleaf,
Breaking Benjamin— yes
I listen that white people shit
while screaming Black Power
I still want my fucking reparations
my idols are Fred Hampton, Malcom X,
Chief Keef, Uzi, Korryn Gaines, Nina
Simone and Toni Morrison
I am not the type to be boxed-in

but ever since you left

I feel boxed-in

locked in the dungeon
of my room like some
princess

I am just as distressed
as my denim
my soul rips at the seams

torn and tattered
healing is deconstructed patchwork

I will be handcrafted
luxury branded
by the time I

am completed. a rarity
a treasure

trove of my own joy
and pleasures
where I won't dwell
over the tethered
memories I wear
as fashion
I wear these scars
like badges

I fought the gym battles with my
demons, shadows
and won the league
I am on my way
to the Elite 4
getting back to my core

this time without you
in my corner
the only affirmation
I need is myself
to know that I am
destined for greatness

Shinigami Interlude (pt. 2)

yet it's empty

trying to figure
out the meaning
of life

when I'm lost in the silhouettes
of what could've been
what I've could've done
to prevent this

chaos has always been my aesthetic
I know black boys
are butterfly effects

it's seems like we're built
to be destruction's incarnate

no matter how gentle
we're always seen as giants

I'm tired of a role
being placed on my gender

I am no Atlas
how they hell am I supposed to
carry the earth on my back
when I can't even keep chemicals
balanced on the axis within my cognition

depression is a Pearl Harbor
and anxiety is guerrilla warfare

and I'm losing because my
communication is broken
bandwidth that's been abandoned
so I'm afraid to make connections
or show the truth of the emotions

I hide behind smiles
I know they can keep the room warm
when my thoughts are the coldest

Gessy 'mae

what is this attraction
magnetic laws that pull
on scarlet threads
as we move raw as marionettes
weaving
our bodies
interlocking
crashing
the cracking
kinetic surges and spasms
our hearts swarm with
butterflies
the effect is chaotic
forbidden
I want to fill her chasm
until it milky ways
remind her that black woman
is cosmic being
celestial body
with a ring around

like Saturn
like angel
even those these
acts we commit
are devilish
I will never condemn her
together we walk a primrose path
until the thorns on our crowns wither

or until she changes her mind
like climate
regardless, I'll
chamber her secrets
with me to the grave

what is this attraction
these tidal waves
we get caught in the current
the present
heat of the moment
but it's more than an instant
it's constant
I want it frozen

in time
so I won't ever
have to
let it go
feels like
I want this to be Eternal
as I Atake her
yet it seems
like I'm the one
who's been abducted
I can't believe
I love the way
she chokes me—

yeah, umm no

would I stop hoeing for you?
I mean, we could hoe together
and create a garden
our own personal Eden
where we can devour
every fruit to our heart's content
fangs in flesh
no shame
society can brand us with scarlet letters
but who cares?
this is liberation
these scarlet threads
that pull us together—

I will always love you

The 10 Commandments of Respecting Kenny

firstly, I do not care
if you accept me but you will
acknowledge me
know that my tongue ain't civil
it's silver
loaded with bullets
you can catch hollows
from these
hallowed words
do not mistake my
offstage aloofness
and quirkinesses as weakness

secondly, open your ears, your hearts and
give me your attention
allow me, to share with you the
tattered fabric
of my soul, the
patchwork of my healing, the
fashions I fathered from my
agony in Tartarus—
I love to show them off like a jailbird

thirdly, give me your honesty
seriously, if I
muster up the courage
to show you a poem
I expect feedback and

constructive criticism
I do not not need a yes-man
who tells me everything is great—
niggas want to grow

fourthly, give me words of affirmation
cast them like
spells from Merlin
that give me
strength buffs—
plus ten to my caliber
keep the iron
sharpened
my pen: Excalibur
pulled from Philosopher's
Stone

fifthly,
sometimes my confidence
can wither
like the ending cusp
of Autumn.
I'm still healing from
past traumas and a broken
heart I wear around
my neck as a choker
like noose
sometimes when I'm numb it
hangs me.
it becomes addictive— at least I feel
something so— please, I

need reassurance
to Spring me back
into my power
realign my spine like
Avatar
remind me that I
am a rock star;
a divine state of being

sixthly, be patient with me
I am a little slow, socially.
reclusively living under rocks
so it's fitting I move like a tortoise—
do not be alarmed
sometimes I
think I'm Mozart
when I make a masterpiece
out of procrastination

seventhly, put your trust in me
my ears and my heart will be a
chamber for your secrets
a safe space for your expression
with no pressure
and I'll remind you
that you are
still a gem
let my
affirmations be spells
that give you life

eighthly, you cannot possess me because
my demons already do— I'm joking...
maybe

eighthly, respect my boundaries
and let me be
free,
Spontaneous
Human
Combustion
of a Sun Sagittarius
without form
I take actions sporadically
doing what the fuck
I want because I'm dope

ninthly, treat me with kindness
and care; I am a treasure
you will not catch me
on social media
talking about,
"I get treated like Fubu"—
no,
I get treated like Versace
I am luxury
and handcrafted

finally, and most importantly
gift me with offerings
of coffee

I have a caffeine addiction
that must be satisfied daily
and I do not run on Dunkin
if it ain't my main dealer,
the green siren
or an independent coffee shop
where I can Instagram
the pretty latte
I don't want it, dammit.
coffee is God's gift
from the heavens
and I must have it

Downfall

it all came crashing
below the bar
of hell
a heart melted like lava
and cooled
into black
igneous
he picks up the broken pieces
attempts suicide
with glass like rock
only to leave abrasions

Hoarder

sometimes I venture into the rabbit
hole of hell
it has become my comfort zone
to pick the scabs of my trauma
like petals

she loves me
she loves me

not

compulsively digging my fingers
deeper into these wounds

I hoard a treasure
trove of memories
I should delete

but the thought of that daunts me—

I'll fight
go to war
to keep these memories
cloaked within a cloud

My Soul is a Shipwreck

I think I'm broken
an error
a stain
on my existence
I'm still trying to figure out
if love is something I'm capable of

it sank the last time
I tried to save it
held my hand
out
pleaded
and
weeped
but I was the one
who sank to
the bottom

of hell

Eternal

as life gently falls apart
I'm gasping, I'm gasping
you left me shattered in misery
I'm gasping, where's my voice?

you kept me at a distance
I'm gasping, have you ever put faith
in the lies you spoke?
*   have you?*

as life gently falls apart
I'm gasping, I'm gasping
you ignored my screams of agony
I'm gasping, I'm gasping

you held me in your arms
whispered it's alright, it's alright
yet your affirmations, were they
counterfeit
or just empty promises?
three years spent with you
I can't believe I lost myself
when did I ever lose myself?

my sanity is severed
why me, how'd it come to this?
you're all I ever wanted
fought for your love, fought for your
happiness
tethered to memories

*hoping they repeat, but they won't
everything has withered, everything has withered
everything has withered, now I'm by myself*

*days no longer change
depression lynches me
hoping I could rewind the hands
my existence is crumbling
days no longer change
depression caged me
because you departed
you abandoned me
yearn to sink into an eternal limbo*

*I don't know? what to do?
when I'm all alone
I don't know? what to do?
I don't know? what to do?
when I'm all alone
I don't know? what to do?
I don't know? what to do?*

Frozen

time for me is
iceberg
sunken
place
a frozen
Atlantis
at the bottom
of oceans
where lost
memories
dwell on the
wreckage of a
severed ship
haunted by a
ghost of regrets

Hoarse

she's the one for me
the only one

I know I should let go
but I'm afraid to forget her

so I hold on to these memories like Neku
lock them deeply within my psyche
and a cloud for safe keeping

no wonder storm clouds
follow me
I reign my own terror
her remnant haunts me
her phantom is a dominatrix
as I offer myself over
willingly to this punishment
caged in this dungeon
within my head
within bondage
I wish our bond never broke
the distance between
us chokes me
silence is the most deafening
sickening my ego
bruised
because I pride myself
on having a voice
but mine no longer
reaches her

How To Mold A Muse

last night, I resented you

        tonight, I yearn for you

    my paramour, my muse
    you are paramount paint

  for my canvas
      the source
      material
      for all my material

last night, I resented you

        tonight, I yearn for you

    tomorrow, I'll mold you
        into Lilith
        portray you as demon
        to hide my own

    weakness
        banish you to shadow
    realm

then revive you from my rib
      title you, *Eve*

      then blame
      all my sins

            on

                you

last night, I resented you

      tonight, I yearn for you

next week, I'll mold you
      into Lilith

      again and
           ask for your forgiveness

    this time
    I will take all accountability
      reflect
         and refrain
    a more vivid
image of your grace

        warmth of your presence
     tranquilizing kisses
  the selflessness of your actions
     that go under appreciated

  I regret not appreciating
     you enough
that regret
    lingers on my tongue

a sweet torment
an eternal longing

last night, I resented you

tonight, I yearn for you

Water Bending

      my tongue is Leviathan

      between her

  thighs. moonlight from underneath
      her   hood

pulls my   tides.

        she be the kindest, most giving

moon rabbit

            producing elixirs

  of life

and my tongue

          is werewolf

to feast
upon her
flesh

black boy plucks petals in the rain

will she ever love me
she'll never love me
you heard her, nigga
and the silence
is her loudest
reply

at this point
you're only telling
your damned self
to wait

with your feet
stuck in clay
you'll mold
your own
grave filled
with regrets
if you keep this up

psycho-self-mutilation

I've always been a dragon
hoarding treasure
so selfishly
you slayed me with venom
from your fangs
sharp as Excalibur
that I treasured
more than my own wellbeing

yet you've always been more crucifix
sacrificing pieces of yourself
that I didn't know how to appreciate
now, I can't find peace within myself

a part of me would love to call it sickening
but I love the introspection
the dismantling of my bruised ego
how I psycho-self-mutilate myself
cutting the very fabric of my soul
I begin to understand
that the melancholic scars on my
melanated body
are stars that form constellations—

I can finally map myself out

seeing more than just the Sun now—
how I relate to the Moon
how I rise with Lilith
where I return to the womb of Venus

I hate to admit that everything happens for a reason
but some losses are Trojan Horses full of blessings

so I thank you
for showing a self absorbed
sheltered soul
a mirror without
rose colored lenses

you probably thought
I wouldn't love myself
when I saw a beast with
eyes as green as Blubasaur
as my reflection

I grew up playing pocket monsters
so I know how to tame my demons
my only weakness is regret

the end of us
felt like the bad ending
to a JRPG
and it bothers me
because *game over*
meant the promise
of forever had an
expiration date

and that was it

The Theatre of Sorrowful Sloth

you are the distortion of my desires

if I had a Palace
it's theme
would be the sloth
of my inertia

my room
is a stage
a theatre
my bed
a casket

where I lay myself
to rest
like vampire
like symbiote
without a host

this is where
I weep
too weak
to take action

in this one man
show
because I lost my greatest
scene partner

now I'm solo
singing soliloquies
as laments
about a living women

I write sins
and my own tragedy

—this escapist genre is fantasy yet horror

Melding, I'm Melting

        I'm not the type to get cold feet

but I panic
at the thought   of you

my desolate heart
    death-races for love
yet, you are so damn   deplorable.

        I want to loathe you so much—
        but all I can think about

        are when your lips are pressed
        against   mines,

        when my tongue sets fireworks

        off in your
                Milky Way

        until you   supernova,

but what delights me most
        is when you are veiled within
    the warmth of my arms,
how perfectly our bodies meld together—

    I hate how my hearts melts for you

Fate Plotted My Torment

my inner demon:
a cruel angel snickers; frost
snarls tormented fate

morning dew

melting between her
thighs

a lava-like   nectar
        that lingers
        on my lips
        sticks
                to my beard

      like morning

            dew

To:

Dear, ▆
I've been dying to tell you
that a part of me still hasn't let go
that I am still very much in love
I pride myself on thinking outside of boxes
but without you I've been boxed-in
by my own cognition
my own mouse trap
a play within a play
inside myself
where I evoke my own guilt
every time I reminisce
and revisit lingering memories
I replay them frequently
like music videos
I memorize them
overanalyze everything that I did wrong
call it self reflection
this perpetual cycle
of my refracted self image
healing
is a refrain
that I have trouble memorizing
(that might be a lie)
I just have trouble
speaking it into existence
because I stumble
stutter over regrets
disguise, "working on myself"

as a means to invoke
green eyes within you
either that
or I just wanted to hear you say
you're proud of me

again

damn, I'm so pathetic
I still think there's hope
at the bottom of my Pandora's Box
just because I cross The Serpent's Path
everyday
I really think I'm Aang
learning to master elements
and balance
but my stakes are just first world problems
however,

I want to move forward

    — love, Buckethead

Mourning Melodies

can you feel his loneliness?
a broken soul so tethered to his past
he walks in ruins
to board a train
that drifts between
earth and hell at twilight
without his rose colored lenses
he sees no difference

alone, he sits amongst
the masses yearning for company
but rejects that notion with his
headphones
loud as heaven's thunder
here, he finds escapism
where the sounds
of gunshots and heartbreak
synergize with 808s
and auto tune
he uses melancholy
found in melodies
as therapy
a *"Death Race for Love"*
as affirmation,
"Skins" as self reflection,
and a *"Sanguine Paradise"*
of low EQ snippets
as self love

Elevate

for too long
you've been fallen angel
a shooting
star
mourning
aimlessly with no destination
lost in the dark
yet still
you are light
and you know it

so elevate yourself
prove that those wings
ain't wax
the sky is your stage
little crow
Crayola all over it

Lover's Block

love poems become the hardest to write
after you fail at the fairytale type of love
you've lost your paramour
now you are in a business of misery
with no company
with no Fairy Tail
powers of friendship
to save you
that ship has sailed, Captain Ahab
this voyage is pointless
you madman

Kenzo's Arc:
Amaranthine Amalgam

Shinigami Interlude (pt. 3)

have you ever had a shinigami
follow you like rain clouds
in the darkest of hours

sometimes I wonder why
it hasn't written my name down yet
why lighting hasn't struck me down yet
I'm always in this Avatar State
I can't control
with no Katara in my corner
so I rage
bending any element
within my range
to succumb the anguish
I go on random walks
just to get away
from loved ones
so they won't have to see the face
of a madman at his lowest

who sits outside of libraries
because they're always closed
for the most insignificant reasons
the most useless of holidays

it's like my Goddess knew
silence was the drug
that's fucking me up right now
because that's all I get from her

I bet a Deceiving God
finds amusement in my torment
how abhorrent
it's leeches itself onto me
like symbiote
I wonder when will my insanity
begin to become a bore to it

have you ever had a shinigami
follow you like rain clouds
in your darkest of hours

maybe if I struck a bell
or scratched nails on chalkboard
it would go away…

if you ever wonder why I'm silent.

her silence. my rage—
a love scar across my face;
bloody wound-blushes

DeMarlo's Lullaby

rinse yourself in tears
until
you fall

asleep

to the tune of regrets

repeat

a lullaby
where the melancholy is tethered
to the melodies

this melodrama
of a distorted desire
the romanticism
of a lover's tragedy and addiction

Phantom (Kenzo)

here I am
armored in midnight
like mourning—

I'm bitter,
sweet like my coffee
yet, still liable to go ghost

Bonds & Severing

side part with   the bang
broken heart lynx   on my sleeve
I'm such a   sad boy

she asked to be my reason for writing but that's impossible. the spot is already taken.

my muse   is a goddess
            who never answers prayers

            foolishly, I   await her return

            writing odes to the source

    of my regrets
            laments of
                    a living Lilith

Cinders

he's covered in ashes
like princess
before the witching hour—
his glass heart
forever lost. frost bitten
and bitter, Frozen Snow
White— he is not Brave
enough to let it go

Sleeping
Beauty away. And wasting
his youth as The Beast of sloth
who hoards himself
in a sea of silence
his only escape is an Ariel
high of astral projection
do not mistake it for balance
he is still Tangled with
his demons

   — awaiting the return of a glass ~~slipper~~ heart

WindScar|Hearts

I hate falling asleep
because I always dream of you

all the anxiety I exorcised
comes back crashing like lightning

again, I'm overwhelmed—
drowning. impulsive.

reversion. my instincts.
chasing after you

like some canine yōkai
wreathed in scarlet threads

these fangs thirst
for your flesh. flirting

with your ghost
no longer quells

my inner storms
as my subconscious rages on

Smōak

it all went down in smōak

you broke it up
I rolled it
perfectly
made it spectacle
because I'm extra

how dare you treat me like a fucking extra

where there's smōak
there's fire
we burned. ablaze.
hotboxed
longer than the rain
forest
as I fiddled
like Nero
Claudius.

under my reign:

I blamed it all on you in the aftermath
like Bush, I didn't heed
your warnings. so I branded
you, *"terrorist"* when I flew
too close to the sun,
crashed into the Tower
of Babel we spent
building together. you cashed out
early on so I was left

to babble in ruins of smōak

Chrysalis

my depression is a state of chrysalis
where my sanity hangs by threads
wrapped in the warmth
of a cloudy sherpa comforter
almost as a warm as the tears
that live stream down my face

I don't ever want to leave

but I know that one day
I must break free from my shell
with my own hands
clawing towards the heavens
with my resolve sharpened
my wings of rebellion
hardened
I will waltz through the sky like a
tempest brewed in teacups
at amusement parks

I would never want to leave that happiness

Crowd Controll

healing is so   frustrating

even on my brightest
sunniest days

there be rain clouds

gathering

in the deepest

darkest

corner of my   psyche

reforming

    molding
      itself into a Trojan

Horse   that I willingly accept

consent   with open arms

   knowing calamity
   will befall me

I don't know if this is depression
      or withdrawals

Forethought

regrets are shackles
and eagles
that feast upon
my insides
daily

rips my flesh
chews and blows
bloody bubbles

in my face
like salt on wound— this wound
shuts
tighter
than my eyelids
only to be split

open
when healing begins
i am back to square

one

Leap, nigga!

if I let go
would i finally heal?
reach metamorphosis?
morph like All Might—y Morphins
and evolve?
go beyond
plus ultra
you'd no longer
be my heroine—
and I'd no longer have these withdrawals

mis. understood

she be mis. understood
she me mist
Hidden Mist
deadly. hit
never miss
she be mis. understood
she be Sierra
Mist
refreshing
she be Sierra
Leone
a bloody diamond in the rough
she be
mis. understood
VVS her clarity
ain't nothing murky about her waters
she be Katara

DeMarlo?

rehearsal is in ten minutes
and i am in the restroom
broken

record, rain cloud
tethered
desperately
trying to pick up
the sandy pieces of me
but the tears keep

                falling,
flowing.pushing.pulling
        washing away the mask
                i am attempting to mold

i do not want to go out there
i do not want them to see

just how broken i am

Lilacs for Lilith

i be hell'a sober
yet i'm an addict
keep all my demons
in heaven's attic

so my storm clouds stay
shrouded
in shades of grey
spewing torrential rain
drenching my essence
but cannot seem to wash
away the hues
of my expression
i am bright
solar beaming
blooming through
the concrete
of my doubts

  —i am lilacs for Lilith

I loved you first, *sticks tongue out

remember when you bought tickets
for us to see a live show for my twenty first birthday
and we made it to the theatre
too late
I knew you were worried
I would think of the date as unpleasant
but I enjoyed every second of it

we wandered about
in Boy's Town
and it meant
everything to me

to escape the clutches
of the winter night we
took refuge in a Starbucks

of course, I always find my way
to the coffee
but

that was the moment

as we sat
at the window counter
deep in discussion

you spoke from plum coated lips

ripened

that's when I slowly
started to fall into the
depths of my heart's chasm
your wide chestnut eyes
stole my heart

I wanted to confess
at that moment
but I didn't want you to
think I was crazy
or being too hasty
but I knew right then and there

I was in love with you

_sandpaperkisses

I give her kisses on her forehead
vitalize her soul
turn her struggles into diamonds
transmute them to gold

she's my _sandpaperkisses
we started out long-distance
slid up in her DMs
the spark was ultra instant
              Ultra Instinct

she's a Leo
so of course
she's regal
beautiful yet
lethal
primal
full of pride
never feeble
yet she moves so subtlety
gracefully and calculated
never formulaic
yet the chemistry
was synergistic
coded in our double helix
she made a nigga feel accepted
not that I was looking for it
know that I'm not normal
she stepped into the portal
of my universe, baby girl
she's the goddess, garden of this world
so I water her

*she's my _sandpaperkisses
we started out long-distance
slid up in her DMs
the spark was ultra instant*

*I give her kisses on her forehead
vitalize her soul
turn her struggles into diamonds
transmute them to gold*

*I give her kisses on her forehead
vitalize her soul
turn her struggles into diamonds
transmute them to gold*

*she's not materialistic
she just want the weights lifted
I should've been her Atlas
but I took that girl for granted*

*damn, I still want her though
my heart cold as snow
it's hard to let her go
but one day I will glow*

*like the sun and shine
and melt this ice
wash away my vices
going up with my prices*

baby girl was so priceless
she cut me like stylus
katana— no mercy
Katara done curved me

I give her kisses on her forehead
vitalize her soul
turn her struggles into diamonds
transmute them to gold

she's my _sandpaperkisses
we started out long-distance
slid up in her DMs
the spark was ultra instant

you're so damn stoic, it makes me sick

while   in   she's
    I'm ruins,

                            unbothered.

flooded her Pearly Gates— now you babble in ruins like a Tower of Babel

Anxiety hugs me tightly and it tells me,

"FLOOD HER SHIT

break the levees of her iPhone
with a tidal wave of bubbles
as blue as oceans

pour your feelings
into each message
finger tips type up
a storm like trident

—and don't think about it
just hurry before you lose her

permanently"

permanent?
we were supposed to be permanent
she said I was stuck with her
now I'm stuck on her

 every time I think I've gotten over her

Anxiety   attacks

and I'm back

texting her

with no reply.

incomplete

my heart

        is

                an incomplete

                          puzzle—

    where the remaining pieces
    are thrown away
    out of angsts
        treated as pawns
            easily forgettable
        because the only
        one who is memorable

      is ███—

Letting Silence Bleed Onto Others

she calls my phone again.
it rings.   and rings.
I watch
with eyes void of life
as another bridge burns.

slowly.
        I just don't want

to answer the phone
        I don't want—
  I'm sick of
    starting over
        this connection ain't

  rare
  this is

    common
    sense

        I only dabble in
          rarities and rabbit holes

of insanity

it rings— I don't want to
to think about shit

       if it ain't ▮—

       "you still stuck, nigga?"

       "yeah"

About the Author

Kenneth D R Coleman is a Chicago based creative who uses poetry and theatre to educate, entertain and empower the world around him. Quirky, with a fearless attitude, he creates a warm, welcoming atmosphere that unexpectedly grows cold through the use of witty bars and politically charged satire that challenges audiences out of their comfort zones.

Kenny started writing and performing poetry in high school where he competed in the *Louder Than a Bomb Poetry Festival.* With a passion for the stage and desires to grow, he majored in theatre performance and creative writing when he went to college at Southern Illinois University Edwardsville where he earned his degree.

All art is political: poetry and theatre are forms of protest that Kenzo uses his to uplift and bring his community together. His craft is also his therapy and it heals— it's an exploration of human emotion and the constant war of being Black in America. DeMarlo's mission is to be inclusive and progressive— to become a voice to the voiceless and marginalized groups— to let everyone know that we all have a voice.

www.ingramcontent.com/pod-product-compliance
Lightning Source LLC
Chambersburg PA
CBHW050913160426
43194CB00011B/2385